THE COUNTRY TREASURY

———

THE WOODLANDER

THE WOODLANDER

JOHN SEYMOUR

Illustrated by Sally Seymour

SIDGWICK & JACKSON
LONDON

First published in Great Britain 1983
by Sidgwick and Jackson Limited
1 Tavistock Chambers, Bloomsbury Way,
London WC1A 2SG

Conceived and produced by
Shuckburgh Reynolds Limited
8 Northumberland Place, London W2 5BS

Designed by Nicholas Thirkell & Partners

Typesetting by SX Composing Limited
Printed and bound in Spain by
Printer Industria Grafica, Barcelona
DLB40832 – 1982
ISBN 0–283–98924–6

INTRODUCTION

PLANTING a tree is one of the very few human actions which can really be called altruistic. A person plants a tree for his children, his grandchildren, or even for their children, but not for himself.

By the accepted standards of our age this is ridiculous. If you cut down a tree that somebody else planted a hundred – or several hundred – years ago you can get money for it. To plant a tree will cost you money and you know that it will never bring you back a penny. What sort of a business transaction is that? What economist, or business consultant, would advise such an investment? What government, that knows its term of office will be terminated in five years, is going to spend money it desperately needs now on something that will not yield a return for perhaps a hundred years?

And yet our ancestors planted trees. That is why our country is so beautiful. Of course they did it on land that belonged to themselves personally, and they all had the dream that their posterity would follow after them and reap the benefit. In a few cases this actually occurred. No tenant farmer ever planted trees. Why should he plant a crop from which only his landlord would get the benefit? Fortunately we have had governments in these islands, in the past, which have been composed of men generous-minded enough to plant trees. The Royal Forests were always preserved, for timber for the Navy; and just after the First World War the Forestry Commission was founded, and by planting trees it served a marvellous purpose all during the great depression employing people who would otherwise have been unemployed, and making use of land which would otherwise have been left abandoned. The country is only now beginning to reap the benefit of this generosity. Can we repay it? How can we repay the generosity of people who are for the most part dead? We can repay it by planting trees ourselves – for *our* posterity.

A little tree-planting is still going on. The Forestry Commission continues, on a reduced scale, bringing more marginal land under trees. There are even, as we shall hear from Bart Vennor in this book, farmers who are beginning, helped by government grants, to plant trees on some of their land. But we are not planting at anything like the scale at which we are cutting down and clearing.

Somehow we must change the human conscience. We must alter the relationship between man and the rest of nature. We must recognise again that the forests are there for their *own* sake – not just for ours. Even if we could do without the woods we have no right to destroy them without replacing them. And we cannot, in the end, do without them.

Surely the test of real civilisation in a nation is whether it plants trees or only just cuts them down. The true civilisation must consider its future. It is not transient. It is only the barbarian who destroys without replacing: who reaps without sowing.

Until about a quarter of a century ago it was very hard work to cut down a tree. Very few people did it. You had to be strong and tough and skilful to swing an axe or wield a crosscut saw. Now the invention of the chainsaw, and various other instruments for pulling out trees, has changed all this. It takes me just a few minutes, with my chainsaw, to cut down a great tree that has stood for two hundred years. It is just too easy. It is no more difficult, though, to plant one.

Happy, and healthy too, were the men who worked in the woods before the chainsaw was invented. They planted and they felled, and they imagined the woods enduring for ever. We shall meet a few of them in this book.

The word "forest" in Britain has several different meanings. It originally meant an area of country preserved for the king, or other important person, for the hunting of deer. Such areas were commonly wooded but by no means always so. Exmoor is an example of a forest with hardly any trees in it at all, and there are several others. The New Forest, and Epping, are examples of royal game preserves, still extensively tree-covered, that were saved from deforestation by the king's forest laws, first applied to preserve deer for the king and his favourites to hunt, and subsequently to provide suitable timber for the king's navy.

The kind of timber most suitable for the building of ships was not at all the kind of timber most commercially desirable today. As Bart Vennor describes below (Chapter IV), modern foresters tend to plant conifers, or soft-wood trees, because the timber from them is what the market wants. The thinnings from soft-wood forests go primarily for pulp wood, most of it to Sweden, for more and more English pulp factories are being closed down. The mature soft-wood timber goes for building construction. Hard-wood timber would of course last infinitely longer but the people of today do not worry about longevity in their buildings. There

are plenty of heart-of-oak or chestnut beams in English buildings that are still perfect after a thousand years.

But in former days it was heart-of-oak that was wanted, and mature beech, for the building of the king's ships; and it was for the growing of such timber that the Royal Forests were set aside.

It was also important that much of the oak should be crooked, not straight. Nowadays the forester goes all out to produce straight-grained, knot-free, timber. But the old ship-builders wanted *crooks*. In a traditionally-built wooden ship there are plenty of timber pieces which are curved, and it is most important that the grain of such pieces follows the curve too. The *hanging knees*, which form the angle between the *frames* (often called "ribs" by landlubbers) and the *beams* are examples of sharply curving pieces. The *frames* themselves are curved, although more gently, the *deck beams* are curved, but more gently still, and various internal strenghtening pieces, such as *sterns*, *stern-posts*, *dead-woods* and *aprons*, are also made from crooks.

Crooks, or *compass-pieces* as they are sometimes called, are grown best in trees that come to maturity in open conditions, not too crowded together. The modern forester, however, crowds his trees closely so that the lower branches atrophy and drop off and the tree grow straight and tall reaching for the light in competition with each other. He only thins when he really needs to. The forester growing ship-building timber, on the other hand, liked his oak trees to grow in considerable isolation, so that they would develop huge spreading branches: park trees rather than forest trees. It was often at the point at which a branch took off from the trunk that a good right-angled crook could be got.

Before the sixteenth century there were plenty of such spreading oaks, and good clean-grown beech to make planking too. But as the navies of Northern Europe hammered each other to pieces, and as more and more timber was needed too to produce charcoal for the smelting of iron for the guns, and for the making of gun-powder, trees began to get short. Pepys, when working in the Admiralty, was constantly calling attention to the need to plant more trees; and John Evelyn brought out his important book, *Sylva*, in 1670, urging all and sundry to plant trees which he thought, quite rightly, were the true wealth of a nation.

The woodlands of Sussex were early depleted, by shipbuilding and for iron-founding. Epping Forest, in Essex, with its predominating hornbeam trees, was coppiced for firewood and for charcoal making. The king's forests of Hampshire (the

New Forest) and Dean, in Gloucestershire, had to bear the brunt of providing timber for the king's navy and did so, as Mr Vennor tells us, until the nineteenth century. At Buckler's Hard, in Hampshire, we can see, preserved as a museum, an ancient ship-yard.

There are still, thank God, some boat yards that use real timber for building real timber ships. Professional fishermen, in particular, want the real thing if they can get it. But more and more such materials as ply-wood, fibre-glass, and even ferro-concrete and "foam sandwich", replace good honest "grown crooks" and pitch-pine or larch planking, traditionally softened by *steaming* so that it could be bent to shape. So the tendency now is to

replace all the open-growing forests with close-grown soft woods, certainly in the Forest of Dean and even, in places, in the New Forest.

There are still many ancient rights, privileges, restrictions and duties connected with several forests. The commoners of the Forest of Dean, for example, are allowed to run stock in the forest, and do so, and their small forest sheep, each marked prominently with its owner's particular paint mark, can be seen wandering about the road-sides. In the New Forest foresters have similar privileges and the famous New Forest ponies, a breed of their own, wander apparently wild, but in reality the property of their owners. Exmoor and Dartmoor, both officially "forests" but without trees, also have their distinct breeds of apparently wild ponies.

Deer, the original *raison d'être* of the Royal Forests, are still plentiful: possibly more so than they were in Henry VIII's day. The Red deer of Exmoor and Dartmoor are still hunted by hounds much as Henry VIII used to hunt them, at least until he got too fat to hunt anything. The Forestry Commission encourages a certain number of deer in many of its forests and employs special people to control them. These latter have to watch the numbers of deer in their areas, shoot some if they are becoming too numerous (to the point that they damage the trees or get out and damage crops in farmers' fields), shoot any sick or weak animals, and generally take the place of the absent four-footed predators.

Red deer, Fallow deer (Shakespeare's "dappled fools") and Roe deer are indigenous to our forests, but Sika and Muntjac have been imported and are becoming more numerous.

The great deer forests of the Highlands and Islands of Scotland are practically devoid of trees now. They were at one time wooded forests but the Scots pine which once covered them was all cleared away to make place for sheep. The Red deer remain and provide sport for the very rich and work for numerous gillies.

But we will start our journey among the wood-landers by meeting one of the old school, Mr Penpraise, who started work in the forests sixty years ago.

MR PENPRAISE

"I WAS fifty years in the forests. I was fifteen when I went in there and I came out when I was sixty-five. I used to look forward going to work swinging the axe – oh yes, I used to enjoy it!"

Mr Penpraise is seventy-four, retired, and lives in an ancient and picturesque cottage at the village of Morwellham, in Devon. Just down the slope from his house is the River Tamar, which divides Devon from Cornwall. Morwellham (pronounced Morwell*ham*) has become locally famous for a museum which has been established there, based on a defunct copper mine, a quay on the river, and various other industrial relics and buildings. Buses and charabancs bring the multitudes down the narrow lane in front of Mr Penpraise's house to look at these interesting things but Mr Penpraise does not let this worry him at all.

Behind his house a bank rises steeply and is heavily wooded with fine trees. This is the heart of the Earl of Bradford's estate and is a famous forest.

It once belonged to the Dukes of Bedford. It is especially famous now because of an entirely new system of forestry being practised there. Mr Penpraise tells how he started his long life in the forests at the tender age of fifteen:

"I was working for the Duke of Bedford then. My father was on a farm. Forest work was hard – harder than it is now. I mean everything all had to be done by hand didn't it? Axe work – no chainsaws. As boys we did paring and trimming round so the men could get in to swing their axes. Just clearing it all back and throwing the branches in the fire – you know, just helping.

"Oh, they were tough men! They were working for twenty-five pence a day, five shillings in that old money. When I started in the woods my wages were fifteen shillings in old money for one week's work, and we had to wait a fortnight before we got any money so it was thirty shillings a fortnight. My father had the same. It isn't like that today. I mean it's better living today isn't it?

"And not only that; since the Earl of Bradford has been here he's introduced piece work – the better the man the better the wages he goes home with. They all got the same before. But the foreman could tell! He would say: 'Come on – you've got to buck up!' They were glad of a *job* back in those

days because if you were out of work – agriculture it came under then – you got no dole money!

"I first started felling trees when I was about seventeen. The only time you had off was Saturday afternoon – you had to work right up to one o'clock. On the Saturday morning the foreman said to me: 'You have got to go with me on Monday morning felling timber.' And he ground up a little axe for me to get used to it. I knew something about it after two years, so on the Monday morning I went and I was all right.

"I soon learned to use an axe left-handed, when

we were stapling or dipping. Stapling is what we used to call it when a tree comes down and you have to trim him down straight so that he will bear on the bench when he goes in to be sawn up. He has to be perfectly round. Stapling wasn't altogether a benefit to us – but necessary when it gets to the mill. A tree without proper stapling, when he gets on the bench, would be more or less cocked up on what we used to call a *toe*. The tree wouldn't be bearing on the bench. [Before felling, the axemen would trim any buttresses or thickness off the base of the tree so as to make the trunk more like a perfect cylinder, so that it would lie straight on the bench when it was to be sawn. This operation was

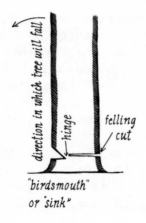

"birdsmouth" or "sink"

of no benefit to the fellers, for it did not help them to fell the tree, but it was most easily done when the tree was standing.] But now they just go round and down with the chainsaw. And the same with dip-ping – they just put the chainsaw in. ['Dipping', 'putting in a sink', 'putting in a bird's mouth', 'putting in a well' are all terms which describe the act of cutting a wedge-shaped cleft out of the tree, on the side towards which you wish it to fall, preparatory to making the saw cut from the opposite side, which will allow the tree to fall.]

"I never did use a chainsaw. The last two years I was on, my mate used to do it, and I used to help with the axe and do all the measuring.

"When you were felling timber in the later years, on piece-work, you had to send in your measure-ments so that they could get so much a cube. That's how they paid. You had your book with the blue carbon paper, you would write it all down, and then you would tear out the page and let the boss have it. Say it was Number One. A Number One tree is thirty foot long and twelve in girth. You nailed a tab on the end of the tree with Number One. Then the boss could come along and measure him, and then look in your book to check it. 'Oh yes, that's right!' he'd say. 'Thirty by twelve.'

"There was one chap who used to work for us who was very straight. He wouldn't try to cheat. But the boss came over to him one day, up to this place called Morwell Down, and he measured the length and said: 'I can't understand it, Norman. Do you know, you were making every tree an inch too big round the girth?' That's a big thing, you know, on quarter girth. Norman couldn't believe it, so the boss took him round and measured it in front of him. Sure enough, it was an inch smaller than what he had down. Norman said: 'I can't understand that! I have never cheated in my life!' So he took his tape out and they put them together. Norman's had shrunk with the weather! 'Well,' the boss said. 'You'd better take this tape and I'd better take that one and destroy it!' Norman wouldn't cheat, although some would try and get away with it!

"To use an axe you can't be a weakling. It's like being a mason – *that's* a cold job in winter time, isn't it? But you get used to it. You had an eight-foot crosscut saw. [The 'dip' was taken out with the axe and then the huge crosscut saw, with a man – and sometimes even two men – at either end of it, was used from the other side of the tree to fell it. The men sat or knelt on the ground to get the saw low enough, for the lower the cut the more timber they got paid for. As the saw progressed into the tree wedges would be driven in behind it to open the cut and take the weight off the blade. It was a final wallop on one of these wedges with the sledge hammer that generally brought the tree down, falling over towards its 'dip'.]

"There were a lot of jobs in the woodlands besides felling big timber. Mr Penpraise owns a peculiar tool made out of the leg bone of an ox. One end is flattened and sharpened, and the other end forms a convenient round handle.

"That's a *rinding bone*, for getting the bark off.

You have a tree standing and you cut him round – six foot high – and cut him down, then you start with this one and lever him off and put your arm round the tree as well. You would get what you could reach off, and then cut him down; and you would rind all the branches and right over the whole tree. When you do you get blue all over your hands, just like ink. I have taken off tons of bark with this tool. When it comes off it is like a pipe. But there is only a month or six weeks when you can do it – when the sap is running somewhere round the end of April into the end of May. It was used for tanning leather. We sent it to Launceton tanner's yard, and we used to have to take off a hundredweight for five shillings. It wasn't weighed until it was dried. You had to save it and dry it like they do hay, then bundle it up.

"At the mill they grind it all up and put it in water, and then leave it until the water is like a pond of ink. Then when they have got a bullock's hide they would put it in there to preserve it. There was no such thing as wellingtons back then – it was all hard leather boots. I always used to wear leggings – the ones with the buttons, you know – to save tearing your legs.

"Getting the bark off was one job we used to do as piece-work [in the Duke's days]. Another was

cutting pea-sticks, and the birch for hurdle jump-
ing – point-to-points and all that.

"The Earl of Bradford has been here since 1959.
I retired when I was sixty-four, about eight years
and a half ago. I was in the nursery then. They
gave you a bit easier job when you got older, and
then I had a big operation and it was just as well I
retired. But I'm fit enough now! I have got my own
chainsaw now. They let me go up into the woods
and help myself to wood. I go up and cut it down
and nip it up with the chainsaw, cut it up into logs
and sell it.

"And I still do a bit of stone hedging and wall-
ing. In the Duke's time everything round the
farms was looked after; if there was a field run up
to the wood's edge the Duke paid for it. He used to
keep that hedge in order. I have done any amount
of stone hedging. The farmer would bring the
stones and they'd say: 'We'll send a man to do it!'
And the same with fencing, and what we call
plashing [hedging by interweaving]."

In the narrow yard between the back of his
cottage and the very steep hillside behind, Mr
Penpraise keeps his motorbicycle (which he still
rides) and his axe. The latter was of the old English
pattern, seven pounds in weight, and bright under
its oil. He will wipe the edge of the blade and

demonstrate that he could shave the hairs off his arm with it. With this tool he has felled some thousands of huge trees.

"The Duke, and the Earl of Bradford, they would supply the tools. I went to a place one day with my brother-in-law, and he had a lovely axe. 'Cor!' I said, 'they don't buy this sort on our farm!' And he said, 'I'll get you one.' Of course, I had to pay him for it. And I have still got it out there and it's more than forty year old.

"So I ground him and took him to work. Mr Kidd – he was our old forester then, the boss – comes up and says:

"'What have you got there old son?'

"'Oh,' I said, 'I've bought myself a new axe.' And I said: 'You never had this sort – the old English sort.' (They always used to buy what they call American axes.)

"Anyway, he said: 'You didn't give all that money for him?' And I can see it now – twenty-one shillings and ninepence in old money! Handle and all.

"So he said to me (mind he was a proper Scotchman): 'I'll pay you!'

"And I said: 'No I don't want the money.'

"He said: 'No – all the other boys are supplied with tools,' and he said: 'I will send the money and

I will pay you for the axe.'

"I said: 'I am not doing it. If you pay me for that axe, whose axe is it?'

"'Well,' he said, 'it is your fault if you will pay for it. What can I do else?'

"I said: 'If you pay for him you can take him away from me and let somebody else have him, couldn't you? You let me have a bit of firewood for him.' Back then firewood was £3 a ton. He sent a ton down here, so I gained on that! Oh yes, it is a lovely seven-pound one."

Does this beloved axe still have the original handle?

"No, but I didn't break him! I had left him leaning against a tree, and we were working on the hill. Suddenly someone shouted 'Look out!' and the timber rolled down, right over the handle, and broke him! So I bought a new one and put it in myself. The handle would have lasted as long as the head if I hadn't had that misfortune.

"The main thing with an axe handle is putting it in properly. The old men showed me how to do it. First, you get the old one out. Then you should push the new one in, making sure it has got a cut in the end of it – push him in and then put a wooden wedge in the cut, to tighten him. If you drive them in, you're *pinching* them! That's what makes them break off! You shouldn't have to wallop them in. Just put them in, easy, and then you get a wooden wedge (I always used an old gate shiver), get him all nice and smooth and drive him in. It's got to be seasoned oak, the wedge. They always say a hickory handle is a good handle."

When some non-experts use an axe, often the head of the axe goes too far and the handle next to the head takes the shock, and either breaks or is bruised.

"We call that 'overthrowing' them. That's the way to break your handle! Mind you, splitting logs is worse for that. I never use my axe for splitting logs, I use any old axe – one that's worn out. As a matter of fact, one that's blunt is better for splitting logs, for if you've got a sharp one he will stick in and if the log hasn't split you can't get him out again.

"I will tell you something else. If you're felling a Silver fir or a Sitka spruce, I wouldn't use my best axe for rigging out [chopping the branches off the felled tree]. That'll bend a good axe – especially if he's very sharp. That'll bend the blade like a bit of butter! Silver or Sitka is very hard, like cutting brass. Where the branches come out of the tree they have a knob round them that's all curly. We wouldn't touch it with an axe! If the knob was a real big lad, we had a crosscut saw to cut him off. Nowadays they don't take any notice of it – they just use the chainsaw. And that's what's making unemployment.

"After I retired, my mate was killed. He had worked in the woods nearly all his life, and I worked with him for twenty-five years. And he was felling with the chainsaw when I used to help him out, as I said: rigging out and measuring. Then I retired and he was working with another chap.

"Working with a chainsaw, you have to wear ear-muffs, and a helmet. One day about three years ago he felled a tree and it went into a fork – a great big one, which split it off – and this fork stuck in the ground and came back at him. He was twenty-seven feet away! His mate shouted 'Look up, Doug!' but he couldn't hear, because he had these ear muffs on and the chainsaw was rattling. The tree came right down on top of his head, and killed him dead.

"Oh yes, they're dangerous things. In the old days you had to be so much more careful; nowadays they are in so much of a hurry.

"Another time I was with a boy one day who was cutting with a chainsaw, and the thing jumped back and he cut his throat! They took him to hospital, and he had it stitched up. He was fine.

"We had a man killed at the mill, once. They had brought a whole load of timber back and they had horses. They took out the stanchion [the removable side-pole that holds the logs in place on the wagon] and there were what we call skids to run them all up. He was doing that when one of the logs rolled down and came right on top of his back."

The woods always were, and always will be, dangerous, and sometimes a felled tree takes its revenge. The chainsaw is the most dangerous instrument ever invented for use in the forest. It has made a tremendous difference to forest labour, and put many thousands of men out of work; but it is not so very much quicker than a pair of really good timber men.

"Two men, whatever they were cutting, could cut two hundred cube a day. But when Doug and I were down there with the chainsaw we would cut five hundred a day. But two hundred with the axe was a nice day's work.

"Three of us once went down to a place called Trecoon, two with the crosscut, and one getting the tree ready – stapling and dip-

ping with the axe. We three cut seven hundred cube of larch! They always used to say of me, 'he's a hard worker!' With larch you could knock the small branches off with your leggings. It all depends what the tree was.

"Another time, two of us went down to this place called Bockdor, and it took us all day to do one little oak right the way through! You couldn't see this tree for ivy, and he was branched out like an apple tree. When he was felled he went right upside down! I felt nervous – you only had to chop off a branch and that was liable to twist her any way. It took us all day to do that one. There was ivy as big as my arm all round that tree!

"When they introduced the chainsaw I wasn't going to buy one, not at my age. I was over sixty. Then I had the operation, and I was taken off and put in the nursery for the last two or three years – looking after the baby trees."

I asked Mr Penpraise whether, if he had his time

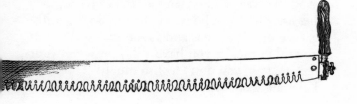

over again, he would have gone into the forests.

"Well, it was either that or going on a farm. If you haven't got any brains for anything else, then you have to do what's there. Not everybody can go into a shop and do their job! It's what you have been brought up to be.

"But it was lovely. I used to look forward to going to work. As you get older you don't want so much of it, that's all. I used to come home, have my supper, and go straight over to the green to play football with the youngsters all evening for hours! I used to play football for the local team.

"I've also done lots of singing. I belong to the choir in Tavistock. It was mostly sacred. I still do it, but it isn't what it was.

"Back in the 1930s a lot of people were out of work. There was no dole. I've never been out of work – not one day! As for holidays, the only day we'd get, other than half a day on Saturday, was Christmas Day and Good Friday! Now it's finished up with four or five weeks holiday *and* odd days in the year. You weren't *used* to a holiday. My father *never* had a holiday. He had to do the milking, even on Christmas and Good Friday. A man once said to me: 'If you have a day off when your wages are low, you don't lose so much!'"

Like all woodlanders, Mr Penpraise practised

many skills in the forests. Faggot-making is an example.

"I bet hardly anyone now knows how to twist a bind – tie faggots. You use anything that will twist, but hazel is best. You take a rod the size of your thumb, and five or six feet long, and twist it. Always keep the butt end under your toe. Then you take the sticks and put them in, put your foot on and pull tight. Then you twist it again. The Duke used to sell my faggots, for fourteen shillings for a hundred faggots. A faggot weighed about 40 pounds.

"Another thing we used to do was make birch brooms. You put the twigs in tight, make a ring, put another one on, tighten, then drive your handle in. There's nothing like a birch broom."

There is a strong innocence about Mr Penpraise, and yet he is intelligent and shrewd. How could a man so gentle have caused thousands of giant trees to come crashing to the ground? But then he had planted thousands more, and trees are like us – they are born to be reaped.

"I love the woods! To me there

was nothing better, and if I ever had a day and somebody asked me where I'd like to go I would say – oh, I'd rather go up Morwell Down or Double Waters than I would go to the sea or anything. I liked to see the rabbits running around, and the birds. I knew a lot of that, but I am like everybody else; I don't know everything."

We may never again see men felling a great tree with axe and crosscut saw. Wherever you go in the woods today you hear the screaming roar of the chainsaw. When I used to wander the woods as a boy I often watched a great tree brought to the ground. You would see two men swinging their axes to a rhythm, swinging apparently with perfect ease, and yet the chips would be flying like huge snow flakes. They would trim the buttresses – "stapling" as Mr Penpraise calls it – and then "put in their sink". Each swinging in turn, they would cut away until they had taken out a wedge-shaped incision about a third of the way through the tree, on the side towards which they wanted it to fall.

Putting down their axes they would then pick up the eight-foot long crosscut saw, which had a handle at each end and teeth an inch long. Kneeling down on each side of the tree they would then start a saw cut at a point opposite to the sink but an inch or two above it. The well-sharpened saw would cut swiftly into the wood. A chainsaw does not go much faster. Then, perhaps, the blade would begin to bind, the weight of the tree pinching down on it. A couple of wedges would be driven in behind the saw with the sledge hammer (never with the back of the axe). Then the sawing would go on.

"Look up," one of the men would say, quietly. There would be no wild shouts of TIMBER like they have in American movies. The two men would stand up. The top of the tree would be moving – very slowly and gently – against the sky. Slowly it would gather momentum, there would be a great tearing and cracking at its base, then a crashing as its branches took the ground first and were smashed and splintered, and finally the great stick would lie among its broken branches and all would be still and quiet.

On the white stump there would be a little fence of jagged splinters. This was called the "sloven". One of the men would trim it off with a razor-sharp axe, for appearance's sake. Then the branches would be slashed off and the great trunk crosscut, with the big saw, into suitable lengths.

The extraction was equally beautiful and dramatic. Somehow a team of huge horses would be led through the woods and hooked to a chain about one of the logs. Leaning into their collars the horses would drag their burden through the under/growth to the nearest ride, or cleared roadway. Here a timber drogue would be waiting: a timber framework on huge wheels. The ones I used to watch, in King's Wood in Kent, had four wheels. Skids were laid up against the drogue, chains were passed from the drogue round the log and back again – over the drogue – and as many horses as necessary were hitched on to the chains. A word and they would go forward, rolling the log easily up the skids. Mr Light, of Brockweir in Glouces/tershire, describes this action:

"Of course in those days when I was young we had timber wagons, and horses. I worked with the wagons pulling timber out and it was hard work.

"You'd get a great big huge log, and you had what we called skids and put them on the wagon and then roll the log up on them. But if the log was too big for that we would wind the chain round the log, have the horse the other side of the wagon, and as he pulled he would unwind the chain and the chain would pull the stick up onto the wagon.

"Many a man lost his life over it. Of course it is safer these days: they have mechanical drags, and they pick the logs up without anyone near and put them where they want on the load. In those days

we had nine horses. We used three horses on each load, but we sometimes had to take two horses off the others to take them back and pull the load up the hill to Tintern Station. Then we would take them back to pull the next load. I've seen six horses there on loads many times.

"We only used one horse to roll the log up, and he would know when the stick had gone over the top, and he'd back back to get ready for the next one."

We shall discuss later in this book why it is vitally important to keep an adequate tree cover over the planet. The quality of the very air we breathe depends on it. But trees can only be planted by the holders of land, and the immediate selfish interests of land holders are not necessarily served by planting trees. It was a common saying in the Fen country of England that when a Fenman sees a tree he runs for his axe. Land that can be growing wheat, strawberries, sugar beet or celery is not as a rule going to be used for growing trees. And the same can be said about cultivators the world over.

Who then is to plant the trees? We shall hear the voice of the British Forestry Commission in due course. It, and its equivalents in other parts of the world, have in fact planted billions of trees. The Forestry Commission plants trees where nothing much else will grow: it does not compete with farmers for agricultural land. But are there to be no trees on good land too?

The tenant farmer will not plant trees. Why should he, when he knows that he will not live, either to enjoy their maturity, or to cut them down? Only the owner-occupier plants trees. He plants for his posterity, and because he knows that he is part of his land, it is part of him, and he thinks of its health and beauty.

Traditionally in England it was the big landowners who planted trees. Most of them were lucky enough to inherit an estate that already had a good tree stock on it, and the best of them harvested the trees as they became mature and planted more to take their places. Every estate had enough tree stock to provide the timber for estate cottages, fences and gates, firewood, and some to sell to the shipyards to help build the ships of the country's growing merchant fleet and navy. As the estates began to be broken up, partly because of absenteeism and lack of interest on the part of the landowners, and partly owing to death duties and other taxation, down came the trees and few were replanted. The commercial farmers who took over the land didn't give a damn about trees. What they were after was money as soon as possible.

Fortunately some big estates remain, and many of these do carry on the tradition of properly farming the woodlands. The Earl of Bradford's estate on the Devon-Cornish border is one of them. And it was on that estate that Mr Penpraise spent his working life and is now spending his contented retirement.

— II —

STAN AYRES

M R STAN AYRES, who lives just across the river from Mr Penpraise, in Gunnislake, Cornwall, was young enough to come in for the chainsaws when they arrived. Stan now works in the machinery maintenance shop on Lord Bradford's estate, having spent many years extracting timber from the forests, first with horses and then with tractors.

"The first chainsaw that ever came out was the Danarm. They were huge things, about fifty-eight pounds in weight. But now they are far lighter, and dead easy to use."

Stan Ayres and his colleagues need to maintain their chainsaws constantly to keep them efficient, however, and mechanical knowledge is as important as the skill with which the tool is used. The engine must be tuned accurately, and the blade needs frequent resharpening. However roughly handled, a well-maintained chainsaw can give years of service.

Various devices are available now for facilitating the sharpening of a chainsaw blade. A chainsaw

is only as good as the man who sharpens and maintains it. But there is little pleasure in working with a chainsaw, it will damage your hearing if you do not constantly wear an ear-muff, it is extremely dangerous, and it is rapidly destroying what little tree cover there still remains. If a man had to fell a great tree with an axe and a crosscut saw he thought twice before he set about it. Now a mere touch of the chainsaw and down it comes.

Stan Ayres began his forest life forty years ago, mainly working on extraction.

"I worked with horses, which were borrowed from a contractor. This was during the war, back in 1943. Horses can be awkward; if you had a good horse you were all right, but if you had a bad one you had to work with him all day. With a good one you could just hitch him up to a stick and he would know where he had to go. The horse would haul the logs to a gantry which was built up with poles. During the war it was mostly pit-props and that was it. [The introduction of steel pneumatic chocks in coal mines has done away with the enormous demand for wooden pit-props that existed until after the Second World War. In those days most of the thinnings of the forest, both of soft and hard wood, used to go down the mines to prop the roof up, and were left there, to rot underground,

— 47 —

as the coalface was driven ever forward.] We would pick them up and stack them on the piles, sometimes as high as six and a half feet. These poles would be up to eight inches through, and anything bigger would go to the mill for planking. If you had a big one the horse would roll him up the gantry, but usually you would have a spike and roll him up yourself. There would be six or seven men working on the gantry, and one horse would keep them going. You would have so many days of felling, and then you would bring one or two horses in and clear that lot out. Then the horses would go off to a different gang that had been felling.

"The timber wagon that took them away would be pulled by two big horses – Shires. An old chap who lived in Tavistock used to do it. He kept his five horses up on a place called the Rock, and he had four Shires and a pony. The pony would go in on the pit-props.

"Clear-felling would usually be done in the summer months, and then we would go back in the winter and replant it. The planting methods were quite different then. You had to dig a pit twelve inches square and twelve inches deep and the older men would come along with a spade and put the trees in. You stick the spade in, turn it, and then put the plant behind and stamp him in and then pull him up so that you get the roots spread out.

"One winter we planted forty acres, which have since been thinned about two or three times. But there is still quite a lot of timber that I actually planted which is actually coming to the mill now. It is not over-big, but it comes in with the thinnings. There are some trees I planted which are growing up to thirty foot high – especially the Notofagus.

"We also cut big oak, and that mostly went for making the bottoms of railway trucks. We used to cut them into fourteen-foot lengths or more, and most of them were the straightest timbers. We used

to load that with the horse and then they went for railway trucks. The contractor, with his truck, lived next door; and he used to come in the evenings and pick it up and take it to the railway station.

"It all goes straight to the Mill now, except the hard wood. We sell that, mostly to Bridgewater. I think a lot of it goes for cover boards and mining chocks and stuff like that. If it's pretty good – beech, ash, good straight oak – it is all loaded on to lorries and taken away.

"I was twenty when I went into the woods, and before that I was working on a farm. It was during the war and I had been called up for the Air Force, but then I was exempt because of farm work. I was exempt for six months at first, and then the farmer got an extension, and finally he got an indefinite postponement. That was fair enough, but if I left or he sacked me I should be called up within ten days. One day we had a bit of a disagreement and I left, or he sacked me, so I had to go and get another job. There was a job going here and I got it, and I have been here ever since.

"My first job was weighing out logs. I would cut them up for firewood. A *mown* is a bamboo basket, like a cotton basket. They hold a hundredweight. We used to weigh the logs and put them in one-ton

or two-ton piles, or whatever the case might be. I was on that job for about five months before ever I saw an axe!

"I went on to cutting down fire wood, coppice wood, planting them and cleaning them out. There was quite a lot of coppice when I first went into the forest.

"I went on from there. I joined a gang that was felling, and of course that was when I started trying to be an expert! I enjoyed that a bit more, because it was something I really wanted to do.

"In those days we took pride in what a stick looked like when it was stapled down and dipped. But today, with the chainsaw, there's nothing like that. We used to cut it down and we wouldn't have any chops! You would have a smooth cut all the way. When you were cross-cutting you would have him level. Today you get a lot of timber in the mill that would still have the bowed end on it, but we never used to have that!

"The bigger the tree the better! If you had to put him down right next to another one, you had to make sure you missed the other one. Sometimes there were several of us the same age working there, and one would go and drive a stick in the ground and see how close he could get to it, see if he could push the stick down into the ground a bit further! These are the things we used to do for a bit of fun, and practice makes perfect! You can always tell if you stand with your legs either side of a tree and look up at the tree and look out to where you want to put him. This is how we used to do it.

"For knocking them over, sometimes you would use wedges but often you would just put your hand on him and give him a push and he would be away. Now they have breaker-bars and things like that. It's a different thing altogether now. There's a bar in the shape of a pinch-bar, and all they do is stick it in the cut – it's narrow enough to go in a chainsaw cut – and it acts as a kind of a lever. On the side they have a turning mechanism that they just shove in the stick [the recumbent tree] and roll him over. We never used to do that – we always had two or three limbs sticking up and a couple of men would grab them when you wanted to turn him and he would turn right over.

"On the felling every man had an axe, a cross-

cut saw, a hammer and two wedges. If you moved
from place to place, all you would have to do was
to strap it on your push-bike and away you'd go!
Nearly everybody had sacks – it was all wrapped
up in sacks so you wouldn't cut yourself. You
would have your hammer and axe tied on the
carrier, and the crosscut tied on the cross bar, and
the wedges would be in your dinner bag and that's

how you would go on the road.

"There were usually six to eight men in a gang. There was stapling and dipping and felling and rigging. Rigging was cutting the limbs off, and usually these were burned. You would have a fire going. If it was hot weather you would put them in perches – that is make long rows of them – and then when it comes to rain you would burn them. They used to use poplar for chip baskets – for the chip factory – because being in the Tamar Valley this area has a lot of market gardening and they needed chip baskets. I have also felled a piece of Sitka spruce, during the war, which went away for aircraft."

So although Stan Ayres never joined the Air Force, at least he helped to supply some of the wood that made the aircraft for it. Like most poeple who have worked hard all their lives in the forests, Stan has an air of fitness and vigour about him, and a kind of quietness and dignity that does not belong to people who lead their lives in more crowded places.

The products of the woodlands are many and various, and there is of course much that comes out of them that is not millable timber. We have heard Mr Penpraise, for example, discoursing on making faggots and witches' brooms, and later in this chapter we shall hear more about the rare practice of charcoal-making.

Certain trees are eminently suitable for splitting, or *riving* as countrymen call it. The Sweet, or Spanish, chestnut is pre-eminent for this, the ash is very good, and the oak can be riven too. Riven timber is stronger, other things being equal, than sawn timber, because none of the fibres that run along the wood are severed. The riving always goes between the fibres, whereas a rip-saw just cuts through them and often across them regardless. Riven wood also lasts longer because grain that is cut off will absorb the water more than grain which is whole and uncut. Riven wood will not be so perfectly straight-sided as sawn timber, but sometimes this is not a disadvantage.

Abraham Lincoln started his career splitting rails. This was the business of riving tree trunks (probably of American chestnut which is now, alas, extinct) down to form fence rails, in a world that had not yet invented cheap barbed wire. The great American barns, which are certainly one of the glories of that country, were roofed with wooden shingles. These were riven slabs, preferably of cedar but of other soft woods too, and I once saw a barn in northern California the shingle roof of which was over a hundred years old and still quite weatherproof. (I saw another such barn the shingle roof of which had been taken off and replaced by transparent plastic, and the barn filled with marihuana plants much taller than I am. Only a sheriff in a helicopter would have dis/discovered them.)

Barrel staves are also products of the river's art. Oak trees are cut, not in England any more but still in Russia and East Germany, and the staves are riven out of them and piled in stacks to dry. These are then shaped with the draw/knife and made into barrels. Clog/makers do much the same thing with willow and alder. Hurdle/makers rive chestnut or ash to make the members of their hurdles. They last about twenty years if kept creosoted and not allowed to drag on the ground. Sweet chestnut would last at least twice as long.

Until recently, characters called Chair Bodgers haunted the beech woods around High Wycombe, and other parts of southern England. Maybe a few still do. These men felled beech trees, rived the trunks, and actually turned the wood to the shape they needed on treadle lathes which they set up in the woods, often out of doors. The chairs that they made were some of the most beautiful, elegant and serviceable artifacts ever to come from the hand of man.

Wood turners still exist in some numbers, and indeed after some decades of decline they are increasing. For example, I knew a man named Mr Ellis, at Boston in Lincolnshire, who was one of the last of the traditional wood turners. Surprisingly (as this was twenty-eight years ago) I recorded some of his conversation on a tape recorder. I bought a *yoke* from him – a proper dairy-maid's yoke such as one sees in pictures in nursery-rhyme books. He made these for the shell fishermen of the Wash, who use them for carrying heavy baskets of mussels or cockles. I used mine for carrying either cans of water or fuel oil to the boat in which I used to live in those days. With it I could easily carry ten gallons of water, five on each side of me; and just try to do that without one!

"I don't reckon turners ought to make those things!" he said to me. "We have to, I know, but it's not a turning job. There's a lot of hard work in them – they're carved more than they are turned. I just make a few dozen a year nowadays – just a few for carrying buckets of milk and carrying sacks of mussels off the mussel stage when the fishermen have a long way to carry them."

True turned work included what he called "working womens' pianos", better known as dolly-pegs. These consist of a circle of wood on the end of a handle with four wooden pegs sticking out of it. The "working woman" stands over the "dolly-tub" with this instrument and spins it round to wash the clothes. The "dolly-tub" is a barrel-shaped metal tub with vertical corrugations in it.

"We use various kinds of English timber," he said. "Various kinds for various jobs. For a

wringer-roller you want a very hard-natured wood such as sycamore, or a maple, or a hornbeam. For dolly-pegs, you want ash. For yokes you want willow, of course. And for the furniture side of the job – chiefly oak, and walnut."

Mr Ellis told me that he felled all his wood himself, or went and got some where somebody else had been felling. He never bought any wood, or very little.

The latter-day wood turner tends to cater for a very different kind of market – not "working

women" with their "pianos", and simple fishermen (if fishermen ever were simple), but tourists
eager to take some curio home from their holiday,
or fairly wealthy people, with good taste enough to
want to embellish their homes with some beauti-
fully grained object of the turner's art.

A form of wood-usage which is rare in Britain,
but which used to be important, is charcoal. I have
seen and talked to no charcoal burner in England
for a long time, but some twenty-five years ago I
met Mr Bill Noakes, in a large wood near Bury St
Edmunds in Suffolk, busily making charcoal. Mr
Noakes had his home, if he did have a home,
somewhere down in Sussex or Kent; but he spent
most of his life living in a trailer caravan, for his
trade was peripatetic.

The particular wood in which I found him was a beech and oak wood and many of the huge trees in it had been felled for timber. Mr Noakes was busy cutting the "slash" (as some forestry people call those branches and parts of the trees which are not timber) into lengths about a foot long and stacking them very closely and methodically into beehive-shaped piles about eight feet high. Over these he placed cylinders, about six feet in diameter, of steel, and covered them with a lid and chimney. These had vents at top and bottom. Leaving both the top vent and the bottom vent that was to windward open, he set fire to the wood at the latter ingress. Very soon the wood inside was a raging furnace and – holding a piece of ply-wood over his face to protect it from the heat – Mr Noakes went in and closed the bottom vent. The fire died out, in time, for lack of oxygen, but he could not open the shell for about a week for it was too hot. When he did open it most of the wood inside had been reduced to charcoal. Mr Noakes had several of these movable kilns in various stages of use.

He told me that a cord of good hard wood produced thirty bushels of charcoal, for which he got a good price selling it to some chemical company. Mr Noakes bagged the charcoal as soon as it was ready. He showed me how you could tell good charcoal by dropping a piece of it on to something hard – it had quite a metallic ring. Mr Noakes, while working, was as black as a chimney-sweep.

I also assisted many times at charcoal burning, in a much more primitive way, in the country that is now called Namibia but was then called South West Africa.

The great world Depression hit South West Africa, or at least white people who lived there, particularly hard. The farmers there suddenly found themselves with virtually no income at all. This did not seem to worry them unduly, for they still used ox wagons, and vehicles called "donkey-mobiles", which were little carts built upon the axles of motor cars pulled by four donkeys.

My own boss, though, whose name was Clinton Andrews, and who owned some two thousand sheep and fifty or sixty cattle, wanted to keep his Model T motor truck going, so he could take cream twice a week into the creamery. He also had an old motor car engine mounted in a shed for driving a centrifugal pump to irrigate his lucerne.

With great ingenuity he constructed two *producer gas plants*, one perched on the back of the lorry and looking like some sort of weird Heath Robinson device, and the other in the shed beside the old car engine. Both worked, and both were fuelled with charcoal. And both, I might say, necessitated taking the entire engine to pieces about once a week to scrape the green tar out of it! Travel in the Ford lorry was sporadic, because every twenty miles or so it would stop and you would have to get out and stoke up the gas plant. You did this by taking a concrete plug out of the top of its furnace. You could always tell the drivers of producer gas lorries because they were devoid of eyebrows. Often, when you removed this lid and peered inside to see what was going on, there would be a minor explosion and off would come your eyebrows again. Somehow, one never learned.

The method of making the charcoal was simple.

The ox wagon, with a team of African workers, was sent off into the bush-veld, and loaded up with wood. The wood was brought back and cast into a large pit. When the pit was full the wood in it would be ignited. When it was burning really fiercely all of us – black and white together – would advance to the roaring fiery furnace each holding a piece of old corrugated iron up before him. At a shout from Clinton each of us would fling his sheet of iron onto the flames. Hopefully the sheets would more or less cover them. Then, each of us seizing a spade, we would shovel furiously. The aim was to cover the corrugated iron with a layer of earth as quickly as possible.

This done, we would leave it all alone for a week, after which the wood would be converted into charcoal and would be cool enough to handle. For charcoal is made by burning wood in an atmosphere starved of oxygen.

It might seem that it would have been simpler to have driven into Outjo, the little town, in the donkey-mobile in the first place, but such are the lengths to which men will go to serve the motor.

— III —

ALEX PETHWICK
AND THE
BRADFORD PLAN

THE "BOY" that Mr Penpriase talked about, who is now "going on sixty", and whose father was Mr Penpraise's first foreman, is Alex Pethwick. Mr Pethwick, too, started as a forest worker, but he has advanced far in the profession now. He no longer sallies out into the woods with an axe in his hand, nor a chainsaw, but sits in a comfortable office back at headquarters or drives about in a Landrover. He drives at great speed because he is a man in a hurry. He has just as much work to do as he can possibly get through. He is a big strong man, as anybody is who started working life swinging an axe, and appears to have boundless energy.

"I have been here forty years, ever since I left school. I have been through the two: the Duke of Bedford, and when Lord Bradford took over the estate I carried on for him. At that time all the felling was done with crosscut and axe.

"My father was in it for fifty years as well. My first job was clearing old scrub, an area of oak coppice. Cutting it for firewood was the first job I did. [Coppicing is the practice of cutting trees down at intervals of several years (generally from eight to twenty) and letting them 'coppice' – that is, grow up again from the stump. More than one stem will arise from each stump (maybe a dozen or twenty) and these will be felled again when the coppice is next cut over. It is an extremely productive way of growing small wood, for example for firewood, posts or hop-poles.] I worked in the saw-mill for eight or nine years and I did a bit of nursery work. I did practically everything. Then I took over. I used to be a working foreman, but when Lord Bradford took over I was given the job as the Forester, on the felling side. I did about nine years on that. I was in charge of all the fellers – the harvesting side of it.

"Now I have taken over the culture side – the planting and breeding. I am in charge of the nurseries. We usually work seven, eight or nine men – it varies. At the moment, with these boys that have started, I have got about ten.

[Alex is talking about a group of boys that had started work in the nurseries under the new government job creation programme.]

"It is hard work, definitely, but I wouldn't change the job for anything! You're out in the country, the job varies, you know you're always on

something different practically every day – and I wouldn't change it for the world!

"The first time I saw anything of a chainsaw was about twenty-five years ago. It's made a lot of difference. Felling trees – big timber – with an axe and a saw is really hard work and I doubt whether many people would stick it like they used to in those days. Now the chainsaw has made the work easy.

"When the old Duke of Bedford had the estate most of the timber we felled was used for work on the estate, for farms and farm buildings. But when the Lord Bradford came we became more commercial. And of course the chainsaw was great for that sort of thing.

"Honestly speaking I don't think you would get the men into forestry if they had to go back to the axe and the saw. The work would be too hard. Forestry's a thing you have got to be born into and you have got to like it or it's no good. My father was in it for fifty years, my grandfather was in it and it

has been in the family, so from the cradle I was brought up in forestry. I think that is what it was and has got to be.

"When I began work first we used to start at about half-past seven and we used to work until half-past five. We used to work on Saturdays until twelve o'clock. You came home tired. For any big timber we used to have a seven-pound axe, which we always kept so sharp that you could practically shave with it. Otherwise you'd be working harder than ever!

"We would put it on a big grinding stone, and get it down fairly thin so the axe would actually *pull in* to the timber, and then finish it off with a smooth stone. We would never use a file because a file would leave too wiry an edge. We would put it on the grindstone about once a month probably.

"I doubt if anyone now could use an axe properly! A real axe-man should be able to use an axe whether it be the right hand in front or the left hand in front. When you are stapling, if you are on the right hand side you would be right hand in front, and as soon as you got on the left side you'd be left hand in front. Otherwise the staple would be on a slant – it wouldn't come level. My old Dad – he used to be foreman – used to play hell if once a tree was down that stump wasn't level!

"We have felled trees anything up to four foot through. I have been so long as a whole day on a beech tree just preparing it to fell for next day, with just two men and an axe. A beech tree has these big staples coming out, and they would have to come down quite straight because to put one on the rack-bench the staple has got to be level."

There is a great art to managing a forest. If you let the trees get too old they will ultimately die, and fall down, and leave nothing but useless scrub in their place. Over-hard felling, however, will leave the estate bereft of mature trees to harvest at some future time. The two world wars played havoc with the forests of England because of the excessive demand for timber. A shortage of mature timber on a big estate can ruin the economy, for the saw-mill must be kept going – its appetite is huge – and the men working in it must be employed. So felling and planting – planting and felling – must go at a proper rhythm.

Thinning, too, is a very important part of the harvesting process. When a block of trees is planted, the baby trees are set very close together so that they will draw each other upwards, straight and tall, all growing towards the light. In perhaps twenty to twenty-five years they must have their first thinning. This will give the ones that are left more space and light with which to grow, but it will also provide useful small timber. In perhaps another twenty years from then a second thinning will do the same and provide bigger timber – some of it perhaps of "millable" size – it can go to the sawmill and be ripped up into planks. There may be a third thinning. After that one is left with a mature stand of timber, the final crop; and nothing is more magnificent (save, perhaps, to stand inside a great medieval cathedral that was built by men for the glory of God) than to walk into a stand of mature oak or beech.

After the earl took over from the duke, and commercial forestry perforce took the place of estate forestry, it was touch and go whether the Tavistock Woodlands Estate could keep the new sawmill going. As Mr Pethwick says:

"There has to be a certain control on it. We are lucky, because the estate is about two and a half thousand acres and we have enough timber on the estate. We have been cutting timber now commercially for twenty-two years, and we could go on cutting for several years yet. And there is stuff now on the estate that I planted – not mature timber, but big thinnings, which is big enough to bring into the mill and be used as timber. That's the Douglas fir.

"As for the small thinnings, we make a lot of fencing materials, for farmers and others, for which we use up our first and second thinnings. This uses up nearly everything we have on the estate, and in fact we buy in stuff. But everything we grow we use in our own mill. At the moment we are only in, say, our fourth crop, so in eighteen years or so we will have hardly enough to keep it going; but after that we should have enough to keep our own mill going.

"I am in charge of the nursery, as I said, and at the moment we do our own seed picking from our own woods. Ninety percent is Western Red cedar. We put it in the nursery and we keep it in the bed about twelve months, line the seedlings out [transplant them] and keep them in the holding bed for say two or three years until they get to about eighteen inches high. Then we plant them out in the woods. I like them from fifteen to eighteen inches high. If you plant them out then they have a fair chance of getting away. If you put them out too small the undergrowth will smother them.

"The fir and pine cones are brought in and kept on muslin on racks. The tiny seeds fall out and are sown in sandy soil in May. When the plants are about six inches high they are lined out. This used to be done individually with each little plant by hand, but now the plants are laid, six inches apart, on a plank, another plank clapped on top to hold them in place, and the two planks, held together, lowered into a trench and the planks withdrawn to leave the tiny trees standing more or less upright."

In another forest, on the Welsh border by the River Wye, Mr Jim Light managed a nursery too, this one for the Forestry Commission. He was the ganger over a small army of women, among the ranks of which was his wife. He recalls the transition to the double plank method of lining out:

"My wife used to work in the nursery, and meanwhile I was the ganger. During the peak season in the summer there would be over a hundred women-folk, besides the men, that I was in charge of. We were sowing the tree seeds, and when they got up so far we took them out and lined them out in rows. When they got to about three years old we raised them up and put them in bundles of a hundred and sent them throughout the Forestry [Commission] all over England and Wales. Wherever the Forestry had land we used to send them the trees.

"For lining out we used to dig a big trench and get down on our knees and line them out using our hands. Then later on they invented the wooden board which meant the trees were all the right distance apart and it made it much quicker."

The late Earl of Bradford, who died in 1981, was a genius and a true man of the soil. He had a lifelong interest in organic farming, and he extended its theories to include the forests. He invented a method of forestry which is quite revolutionary, and which no doubt will one day become the accepted practice in all temperate forests.

The forestry commissions and departments of this world practise a very simplified kind of forestry. They clear-fell an existing forest, or else deep plough a piece of open land, and plant trees, all of one species, and all of one age. In due course they thin, then thin again, then possibly a third time, and then they clear-fell. This clear-felling may take place anything from 70 to 150 – or even more – years from the time of original planting. This method of one-crop one-age planting and clear-felling has the advantage of extreme simplicity, and anyone can understand it.

The best private foresters, though, have always practised a much more difficult and subtle art. They manage forests of mixed ages and species. They encourage, as far as they can, natural regeneration. They like the trees to seed themselves. But such forestry can only be practised by very skilled and knowledgeable men, who have a real sympathy and feeling for the work they are doing.

The first method, one-crop one-age forestry, has the disadvantage that it lays the forests wide open to disease. Monoculture – the growing on land of only one species of crop – always leads, in the end, to disease. For the disease organisms that attack that particular species run riot eventually and wipe the crop out. This is already beginning to happen in the big monoculture forests that have been planted in the past fifty years. In America and elsewhere great programmes of aerial spraying of poisons are being carried out, but these – besides having woeful side-effects – are not proving very effective. This monoculture of trees even *looks* wrong. Rows and rows of regimented conifers spreading over the hillsides, all the same species, all the same height, just look ugly. A side-effect that commercial foresters do not have to worry about, of course, is that such forests are the home of practically no wildlife. As a habitat for other plants, birds, mammals or insects, they are about as hospitable as a desert.

A further disadvantage of this form of forestry is that strong doubts are beginning to arise as to how long it will be sustainable. Observations in Europe, where such methods are older than elsewhere, have shown that after two crops of conifers have been clear-felled the land is not fit to produce another crop of conifers. Nor is it fit for anything else. The acid and depleted soil is sterile, and it might take centuries before it will grow any useful crops again.

A mixed woodland, and a mixed-age woodland, does not have these disadvantages. There is no great stretch of trees all of the same species for some pest or plague to run through like a forest fire. The leaves dropped annually by deciduous trees add life and humus to the soil. The best agricultural land in Europe was formed by the mixed forests of the past. Furthermore, a mixed-age mixed-species forest can be very productive. Different species of trees help each other. They take different things from the soil and put different things back. Some provide shade for small trees and act as nurse-crops to them. And of course, if anyone is interested in such things, they provide a magnificent habitat for other forms of life and are incomparably beautiful.

So the sixth Earl of Bradford – together with his Forest Manager Phil Hutt – devised the "Bradford Plan". This is simply an attempt to reduce to rule-of-thumb the extremely difficult and variable art of managing the mixed-species mixed-age forest.

You go into the forest and pace out a square twenty yards by twenty yards. You can use a pacing

stick, but most men of normal size can pace a yard out exactly without thinking about it (which is why a yard is a better measurement than a metre). You peg this out and stretch string between the pegs. Then you subdivide this square into nine subdivisions. Each of these sub-divisions will be, owing to the fact that there are three feet to a yard, twenty feet by twenty feet.

You go to the middle one of the nine sub-divisions and fell all the trees in it, large and small. You clear-fell it. (If it starts off by being bare land, of course you don't have to do this.) Then you plant *nine trees* in it. As Alex Pethwick says:

"We nearly always put in a shade-bearing tree: Western hemlock or Western red cedar. Now we leave that for six years.

"Six years later we go in and take out another twenty-by-twenty foot [sub-division]. We go which way we want to go – we may choose north or south – and we do exactly the same thing. Now every six years we go round and as soon as we get to the last one of the nine the first plot is forty-eight years old. So when you are planting the last square your first one is mature timber.

This sounds more complicated than it is. Just imagine that you have nine squares – all in a big square. You clear-fell the middle one and plant nine baby trees in it. We will call that Square One. In six years time you clear-fell another square – it doesn't matter which one – and plant nine baby trees in that. We will call that Square Two. Six years later you clear-fell Square Three and plant nine trees in that. Six years later you clear-fell Square Four and plant nine trees in that.

Now when you plant up Square Four the trees in Square One are eighteen years old, so you may decide to *thin* them. You might take out three or four of the nine trees in Square One. Then, six years later, you plant Square Five and thin Square Two. And so on. Then maybe six years later, when you plant Square Six, you may do a second thinning in Square One. You conduct the thinning so that, forty-eight years after the first planting, there is but one tree left in the twenty-by-twenty feet of Square One and that tree is ready to fell. At that age the growth rate of soft-wood trees slows up and, for the most productive management of the forest, trees should not be left to grow much older.

Then what do you do? You are left with Square One bereft of the trees you first planted. But there has probably been natural regeneration, and a lot of small trees have grown from fallen seed in the now-cleared Square One. If so, you thin them down until you leave nine trees again. And the

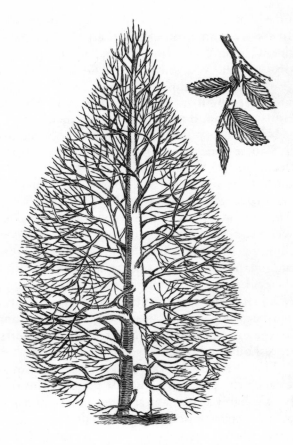

Notofagus or Southern Beech

cycle begins again: just one complete cycle in a man's natural working life span. Your grandson should see the completion of the third cycle. If there has been no natural regeneration, you would plant nine new trees, of course.

The Bradford Plan is designed principally for coniferous trees, but it has already been adapted to hard-wood trees, some of which were planted within two years of their start. Alex Pethwick explains:

"We have experimented with some hard woods. Lord Bradford himself brought over from South America the Notofagus – the Southern beech. We have put the Notofagus as the central tree in each plot, and of course we thin around that one. We are geared up at the mill for all soft-woods, but we also plant a certain amount of hard-woods like Notofagus. We even have open areas here with nothing but Notofagus in, pure stands of Notofagus.

"Of course we still don't know whether it is good enough for timber. We think it will be, but we haven't anything that is big enough yet really to tell what sort of timber it will make. What we have cut we sent away to the brush people, and we have had a very good report back. They say they would use as much as we can supply. But at the moment we haven't got anything big enough to fell. The oldest is about twenty-two years old – a tree in the region of sixty-five feet in twenty-two years, whereas the Western Red cedar planted about the same time is only about twenty-five. If the timber is proved to be good, then this tree is definitely going to take the place of the elm."

I myself have seen Notofagus twelve years after planting, in the Kennedy Memorial Park in Ireland. They were fine big trees – twice the size of any other tree, hard-wood or soft-wood, planted at the same time; well shaped, straight, healthy and good looking. This could undoubtedly be the commercial tree of the future. The present genera-tion of foresters will probably have to retire first, though, and make way for new ideas, before either the Southern beech, or the Bradford Plan, will be taken seriously in the commercial forests of the world. Meanwhile the Bradford Plan forests in the Tavistock Woodlands Estate, first started in 1958, look delightful and highly promising. For the first time someone has reduced to a rule that anyone can follow the intuitive forest culture of the past.

BART VENNOR
AND THE
FOREST OF DEAN

ANOTHER most enlightened forester is Bart Vennor, who works for the Forestry Commission in the Forest of Dean.

"We plant trees in the hope that, by the time they are either thinnable, or mature for felling, we have a market for them. We have to look for changing market forces while the trees are growing.

"There is a tremendous market for hard-wood at present, but it depends on the size and the species. We hope that people will always want long-lasting furniture, and solid hard-wood furniture is probably the best there is. If you want a suite of oak furniture you can go to the local shop in Monmouth and buy yourself a three-piece suite for £2,000 or more. It will certainly last three or four hundred years – as long as people don't put it too close to modern methods of heating! If that's what people want, and I hope they do, we will always have the need for fine grown oak and beech to provide good long-lasting furniture; and for sycamore and walnut, because people like to see fine figuring on their bookcases and pianos. There will always be a need for hard wood.

"But of course one's life can't be measured by the life of a tree, and if we live to be three score years and ten we will only be perhaps half way through the life of an oak tree. Other hard-wood trees, like ash and cherry, grow to that length in about seventy years. People often ask what use is cherry? But then there are always people who smoke pipes! It also has other uses because of its fine colour; it is used for coffee tables and that sort of thing. There is an ideal cottage industry for people in this area if they are prepared to saw it and season it and make small furniture from it. It's a tree that grows very well in the wild, and it is a natural tree in the Forest of Dean (as is the lime tree). Cherry also has high amenity value because it comes out in flower in spring before it comes out in leaf, and you can say to yourself: 'Good – it's Spring!'"

Bart Vennor is a long, lean man, who has spent his life in forestry, and whose job now is going round advising landowners who want to plant trees, and who want to get grants from the Forestry Commission to do it. He has a missionary zeal. He really wants people to plant trees. He realises, I believe, that a land without trees is a desolate land, and a people who do not plant trees are an uncivil people.

"Many farmers in Gloucestershire are turning to buying woodlands or planting up areas of their farms on which the return from agriculture is not very high, knowing that the trees will provide them with something. Certainly farmers are beginning to replant where over the last twenty years they have probably been clearing – to try to increase their agricultural holding.

"Because of the grant system some of them will plant hard-woods, but of course they do mix in some conifer because they can take out young thin-nings for posts and stakes and the like to see a return in their lifetime: and who can blame them? In Gloucestershire we would probably not pay them a grant for pure conifer, because pure conifer is not appropriate for the south of England. We would accept a mixture, and the County Planning Department would accept a mixture. The Forestry Commission would pay a grant on a mixture anyway, so the farmers are quite happy to mix the forest up, some conifers and some hard woods.

"The long-term effect in the country will be that the hard-woods will still be there in something like the year 2200 before we know if our plans now are right. And we won't be around for anyone to tell us that we were wrong.

"At the moment I'm doing private woodlands advisory work for the County. Having spent twenty-five years working in the Forest of Dean they let me loose at last! I don't use any *persuasion* – apart perhaps from the gift of the tongue, which stems from my grandmother's side!

"I think people are beginning to realise, since

the loss of the elms, that there is a real value in having trees. As they reach maturity people remember their childhood, and they look back across their fields and say: 'We used to have rows and rows of elms. They've gone. What can we put in their place?'

"Often they decide that, rather than just having hedgerows, it is better to block off corners of fields – because mechanical agriculture needs round fields rather than a square. They round off the corners of their fields and they make a woodland. That could be grant-aided, either by the Forestry Commission or by the Countryside Commission, depending on its size.

"The Countryside Commission grant-aid the replacement of hedgerows, so if they want to put in the equivalent of the old type of hedge, in place of elm they would put in ash or sycamore or whatever species suits the land best. They get a grant for that.

"In the County over the next thirty-five years we should see the revitalising of individual standard trees, and hedges. That can't be bad because it sustains the wild life. It's easier for the wild life to move along hedgerows than it is for it to move along barbed wire fences. I think we're seeing a reversal of the common recent-past type of agriculture, where you knocked out all the hedges to make larger and larger fields. I hope it is stopped and is going into reverse. The reason is that grants are available, and because pressure is being

not only by conservationists but by people who accept that perhaps we were wrong in making fields larger and larger. Although we find it easier to harvest a lot of land at once we still get erosion. It may be on a slightly smaller scale than they have in America, but we do lose soil in this country – by wind or by rain erosion – and people argue quite strongly that Small is Beautiful!"

There is great controversy over the question whether soft-wood or hard-wood trees should be planted. Foresters tend to plant soft-woods because soft wood is what is wanted. The huge amount of building timber that is required by an ever-increasing world population is nearly all of it soft-wood. Fortunately, for those of us who like to see the traditional hard-wood trees of the British Isles, recent governments have also been showing a preference for deciduous trees.

"Oak is still being replanted in the Forest of Dean, and indeed last time there was a ministerial statement on the Forest of Dean, in about 1971, it stated that of the twenty-seven thousand acres in the Forest of Dean half would contain a hardwood crop for ever. Thirty percent would be mixed hardwood and conifer, fifty percent would be mixed hardwood, and twenty percent would be conifer. In a hundred and fifty years' time there should be eighty percent hardwood [because you will have thinned out the conifer mixed in it]."

I asked Bart Vennor if he could explain the extraordinary fact that Britain, which has very few trees, and Ireland, which has even fewer, are at present exporting much of their timber to Sweden, which has a lot.

"Well, the thinnings used to go for chip-board in this country, but now we no longer have a chipboard industry. Over the last three years we have seen the loss of some two dozen pulp factories in this country. So now we have to look for different outlets for the young conifer. We can't say to a plantation: 'I'm sorry – we don't need your trees! Just keep on growing!' because naturally they will kill the rest off and we will lose the value.

"Sweden is covered with trees – about seventy percent wooded and thirty percent laked. I don't know where the people live! Either on the water or under the trees I suppose! But their trees grow much slower than in this country. We grow trees three or four times as fast as Scandinavia and twice as fast as they can in France or Germany. So if the Swedes go on cutting down their trees they will be doing themselves out of timber. So it would appear that what they did was to subsidise their pulp production by providing cheap energy, and of course their energy is cheaper because they use hydropower instead of coal. That's how they can produce pulp and chip-board at a more advantageous rate than we can in this country.

"They set their sights on the fact that we grow our timber more quickly, and therefore they can come to us for timber while they are not only keeping their forestry in good production but their work force in high production too. You only have to look at Bowater at Ellesmere Port: they have put eleven thousand people out of work within the last couple of years! And that's only one factory. Now *all* the manufactured pulp-wood comes from

Scandinavia. We are putting our people out of work to keep their people in work!"

Bart also speaks of a new and expanding market for forestry thinnings and, particularly, for the thinnings of hard-wood trees, or for the slash, or small branches of them, which would hitherto have been wasted – burned where it was cut just to clear it out of the way.

"The manufacturers of wood-burning stoves tell us they sell about fifty thousand wood-burning stoves a year. When they sold the first one wood was cheap, but when they sold the second one there was competition! If the people who buy them use them for heating and cooking purposes, a three-bedroomed house with a wood-burning stove in it would need about seven tons of wood a year – and that is *dry* wood! Fifty thousand wood-burning stoves a year at that rate would consume three hundred and fifty thousand tons. If that goes on for long we will only be producing wood for the fire-wood market!

"If we could find a hard-wood that would grow more quickly and produce the firewood, then fine. If not, we will have to return to the conifer. Conifer burns in wood-burning stoves in exactly the same way as hard-wood, so long as it has been stored for eighteen months before the fire being lit. All wood needs to be dry, but with the resin in conifer being more highly damaging to the flue – so that you can set the chimney on fire and perhaps burn the chimney out – you must make sure conifer is *totally* dry before you put it on the fire.

"What will stop the sales of wood-burning stoves in the long run is that people will find it is very time-consuming. They have two choices: either they have their own wood, which means they have to go and cut it; or they don't have their own in which case they have to buy it. It is a well-known fact that you will probably get four warms out of your fire! You get warm when you are cutting the wood down, you get warm when you

are splitting it up, you get warm when you are sitting in front of the fire, and you get warm when you are carrying the ashes out!

"In the short term I think wood-burning stoves are a wonderful thing because they are providing the forester with a means of getting rid of his waste wood.

"Firewood, delivered, is probably about a third of the price of coal. It is currently about £50 a ton in the New Forest, and as little as £30 a ton delivered in Gloucestershire.

"Twenty acres of coppice should sustain your house for ever. If you are in a wet area you will over-produce with this, because you can coppice alder or poplar which will grow very quickly. Coppice alder can probably be cut over every eight to ten years. You should grow the species that are natural in your country. If you are on drier land, of course, it will grow more slowly but it will produce more heat because it is dense; so you wouldn't be chucking so many logs on as if it were poplar or alder.

"If I had a free hand I would forest all the land I could! It is well known that the world stock of wood is diminishing at a great rate. We use it and we waste it every day. But there are certainly a lot of areas that are available for woodland which are still being wasted. In this country we still have something like ten million acres of land which are not being used. I would certainly argue that growing timber is better than growing grouse, or anything else, on those hillsides.

"If we cut down more and more of the equatorial forests as we are – because of the greed of the people who own the woodland, people who often don't even belong to the country where the woodland is growing – it must upset the balance of nature. We actually need the trees, for our own oxygen consumption. So I shall certainly go on advising more British people to grow more wood on their own land. And I shall try to prove to those people in other countries that they ought to be looking after their own."

Mr Vennor's own forest – the Forest of Dean, in which he lives and in which he spent most of his working life – is like a good deed in a naughty world. It seems like a little sylvan world of its own. But it has its ups and downs.

"It has had a very chequered history, and you have got to go back to the 1600s to know the full truth about the Forest of Dean. Sir John Winter, Admiral of the Fleet, was a local landlord who was owed quite a bit of money by the Crown, but because it was war-time they couldn't pay him. So he suggested that he went back and looked after the Forest of Dean. He came back and reckoned that if he felled the Forest he would make the money that he felt the country owed him for being Admiral of the Fleet.

"This is what happened. He felled it almost totally, and it is recorded in Pepys' diaries that not only did Winter fell most of the trees but that a wind blew for three days and flattened what was left of them! That was in about 1680, I think, as history records it.

"Pepys, on one of his tours of the country, came to the Forest of Dean and sent a report back to Parliament saying, 'you know what that Winters has done – he has felled the Forest of Dean!' And Parliament then took over the Forest of Dean and it has been in Parliament's hands since the late 1600s. It has been run as a state forest since then.

"After that it was always felt that because we were making wooden war ships, and the wooden warships were always made of Dean oak, Dean beech, Cotswold beech, Sussex beech or what- ever, so every time you felled a mature crop of oak or beech you would replant it so that you had a continuous supply to replenish the Navy. The last wooden warship – or the last lot of timber sent to the Navy – was from the Forest of Dean in about

1884 or thereabouts."

The driving need for hard-woods to build war-ships, that were constantly being battered to pieces on the high seas, and which so troubled Pepys, is no longer there. And when a landowner – includ-ing the Forestry Commission – can get two or three profitable thinnings and then cut a mature crop of millable soft-wood in fifty-five to seventy years, whereas he or it would have to wait a hundred and fifty for oak or beech, the temptation must be there to plant conifers. Fortunately some people resist this temptation. I knew a Mr Davis who owned a saw-mill at Bucknell, in Shropshire, who planted in his life hundreds of acres of walnut. This would not be ready to cut down for three hundred and fifty years. When I asked him why he did it he replied: "Our ancestors planted walnut for us – it's right that we should plant some for our descendants."

The late Fritz Schumacher believed that it was permissible to cut a beautiful tree down if you were going to make something of the wood which would be beautiful too, and which would outlast the natural span of the standing tree. Alas, most of the forests of the world are now being cut down to make newspaper, wrapping paper, chip-board and other items that are neither beautiful nor long-lasting.

As Bart Vennor pointed out, the small traditional sawmills of Britain are at present in the
doldrums. Nobody can compete with the Scandi-
navians and Russians for soft-wood ("deal")
processing, and Swedish competition has also
closed down the whole British pulp-wood industry.

Some small specialised hard-wood sawmills
still exist, however, and Mr Thomas, of Cilgerran
in West Wales, describes why he has had to stop
milling in his own once very successful and long-
established sawmill.

"Some years ago I think we employed twenty
people, and we were very much geared up to a
production run. But our equipment is a bit
ancient; it was all bought by my grandfather. The
economic fact is that we haven't been able to make
enough profit to replace the equipment.

"We used to buy all the timber locally. The
farmers would phone up and say they had a
certain amount to sell, and we would go out and
give them a price for it. We had our own crane and
a lorry, and we used to have four men ready to
bring it into the yard. In a day we would bring in a
load of timber, about two hundred cube, and cut
it in the same day as well.

"When the timber came in it went through a

large band-rack, the kind which is used a lot in Canada. The table is the rack bit which actually moved, pulled by two pulleys, and there was a great big band saw. We also had another large saw, a circular rack, which had a great big blade of about five feet in diameter, and that cut the timber down initially. It was quite wasteful, really; we used to reckon a wastage of about thirty-five per cent, by the time you had taken the first cuts so that you could turn the log and get it even, and then you had to keep on taking slabs off it. Oddly enough, one of our biggest problems in those days was getting rid of the fire-wood. This was before the days of the wood burning stoves.

"We had about ten men working in the mill then. Most of these had worked with my grand-father, old timers. First the wood was cross-cut into lengths with the chainsaw. If we were cutting stillages of thirty-six inches with a chainsaw then it went on the circular rack which cut it down and took the slabs off, then it went down – on a dram on rails – to another saw which cut it down to one regular size, such as $2\frac{3}{4}$ inches. At this point all these blocks then were $2\frac{3}{4}$ inches by twenty. Finally the blocks went through another saw which cut them down to the finished size. We ended up with timber that was 2 by $2\frac{3}{4}$ inches and varied in length

from twenty to thirty-six inches. These were then
stacked in blocks of about three hundred. Once a
week we used to send a load off to Lampeter sawmills or another manufacturer in Swansea, where
they converted what we sawed into pallets: they
made them into pallets mainly for the steel industry.
The biggest problem was that the steel industry
controlled the price and they were very ruthless
people to deal with.

"There was a time when the one great boom for
people like us was figured sycamore, which was
used for furniture making. But whenever we came

across some my father used to sell it in the round. The nearest we ever got to selecting was actually selling the timber.

"The band saw, of course, could cut far more accurately than the large circular saw, but in our mill it was mainly used for cutting oak for fencing posts and that sort of thing. It was slower, but I don't think that was the fault of the saw – the people were geared to using it at a certain speed and they didn't want to change. The circular saw was faster but not so accurate.

"We would occasionally get an order for soft wood pallet boards, but other than that we couldn't sell it. Anything we sold locally to farmers used to be oak, but this has changed completely now; everybody has given up with oak and we sell soft wood fencing posts and people don't mind at all. On the builders' merchants side we sell a lot of imported timber, but of course that is a lot dryer and seasoned. With local timber you couldn't actually cut it up and sell it as roofing timber, or what have you, without seasoning it to a certain extent.

"There is a British sawmill cutting up British spruce and other soft woods, but the quality isn't very good and we had a lot of trouble selling it. It was unseasoned and tended to twist and turn; and the sawing itself was poor, although I believe that the sawmill cost three million pounds. One day we may come round again to using our own timber from the forestry plantations that are coming up. But it will be a long time before we can sell local timber to builders.

"With British-grown timber the marketing needs to be sorted out; and it needs to be seasoned more. We could do it, of course, but there is no one actually doing it. In Sweden, on the other hand, things are quite different. I have seen sawmills there which cost around thirty-two million pounds, employ five men, and produce as much timber in a morning as we used to produce in a year. It was incredible. I cannot see how we are going to compete with it, or who in this country would be willing to invest that kind of capital to produce what is, at the end of the day, a cheap product.

"In this Swedish mill everything is computerised and automatic; the timber is never touched by human hand, and the operators wear ties and collars and even suits. They simply instruct the computer in the morning that, for example, three-by-two timber is to be cut, and anything that cannot be economically cut to this size is automatically rejected, and stored to be cut to a different size later. Every log as it comes up to the blade is automatically moved into the optimum sawing position; and the sawdust is channelled off to be made into chip-board. With a system like this there's absolutely no wastage at all.

"In the present climate, and against this kind of competition, I don't see much future for sawmill businesses like ours. The only way sawmills would have a future in this country is if we subsidise them. We're not going to invest the kind of capital needed to build a modern sawmill – five million at least – when as merchants we can buy the stuff so easily and cheaply abroad."

My own first glimpse of the workings of a saw-mill was in the Makushi forests of Barotseland, in the country now called Zambia. We used to call it Northern Rhodesia and it was then a British crown colony.

My work as Livestock Officer for the Northern Rhodesian Veterinary Department made me responsible, among other things, for the health of the cattle which belonged to the Zambezi Saw-mills Company. The latter owned some six hundred oxen to haul logs out of the forests and, as the whole operation was typical of tropical extrac-tive forestry, it might be of interest to describe it.

The Zambezi Sawmills Company operated from a place called Machili in the Sesheke District.

Machili was connected to the town of Livingstone by a privately owned railway a hundred miles long.

Machili was situated in heavy bush country in which grew, scattered here and there among the other trees, very big trees called Makushi, or Rhodesian Teak. Into these forests the loin-clothed lumbermen would go, armed with nothing else except their small native axes – simple blades of steel stuck in a knob of wood, and a crosscut saw. They worked in pairs, and each pair could knock off work when the two men had felled one tree of a certain size and cut it up into logs. The logs were exactly the same length as railway sleepers.

When a pair of loggers had felled and cut up their quota they set up a terrible cry. This would call, eventually, a man called a "boss-boy" who would measure their work. If it was sufficient he would sign their card and their day's work was over.

Then in would come the oxen, working in spans of six or eight, and the span would be hitched on to an enormous log and would drag it out of that block of forest to a light railway line. It would then be loaded on to a rail truck and taken to the sawmills.

There it, and hundreds of others, would be greeted by a circular saw with an eight-foot diameter blade which was called "the breakdown saw". I used to stand, sometimes, in a small glass cabin, beside the man who operated this, and watch him with considerable awe. A huge log would be levered by Africans from a truck on the railway on to a moveable platform. The white sawyer, who could not be heard by anybody out-side the cabin because of the whine of the spinning saw, would signal to the Africans by various esoteric signs of his hands. Acting upon such instructions the team would lever the log around until it was in exactly the position required by the sawyer.

The latter would then pull a lever over to his right. This would set the platform, with the log on it, in motion towards the saw. The log would be carried – at what seemed to me a terrible speed – towards the spinning saw, end on. When the end of the log was an inch or two away from the saw the sawyer would right the lever and stop the log dead. If he had failed to do this at the appropriate split second the log would have crashed into the spinning saw at top speed and, I imagine, completely wrecked it. Then, moving the lever more gently, the sawyer would bring the log in contact with the saw and an ear splitting scream would be set up. Slowly, inexorably, the log would travel from our left to our right until it was ripped right down, into two. The lever would then be flung the other way, the platform with its log would slide swiftly to the left again, out to where the team of log handlers waited, with long levers, peevies and crowbars, they would shift the two halves of the log about, acting to the sawyer's signalled instructions – and then the process would be repeated.

The result of all this would be that the log was cut into railway sleepers, and at that time all the railways of Southern Africa were laid on Makushi sleepers from that sawmill.

In contrast to this I have often stood and watched, in Africa and in Ceylon, pit-sawyers at work.

In many of the traditionally-wooded parts of England you will find, if you look, a pub called "The Top Sawyer". I have never found one called "The Bottom Sawyer" yet. The sad truth of it was – to be a Bottom Sawyer was not a very enviable job. But most of the wood that went into everything made of timber, in days of old, was ripped down by a Top and a Bottom Sawyer.

There was a pit in the ground. Over this long pit was rolled a tree trunk. Down into the pit got the Bottom Sawyer. Up on top of the log got the Top Sawyer. Between them they had a long rip-saw. A rip saw is a saw with very slanting teeth and is for cutting *along the grain* of the wood only. By contrast a *crosscut saw* has straighter teeth and is for cutting across the grain of the wood only.

The Top Sawyer would grab the wooden handle at his end of the saw and pull it upwards. The Bottom Sawyer would grab the handle at his end and pull it downwards. They would alternate doing this all their working day. The Top Sawyer was up in the sunshine and, above the rasping of the saw, he could hear the birds sing. The Bottom Sawyer, by great contrast, was down in the pit and he could neither see the sun nor hear the birds sing. Above all, every time he looked upwards he got an eyeful of sawdust. He was showered with the stuff all day. You probably had to work twenty or thirty years as a Bottom Sawyer before you rose to the dizzy heights of Top Sawyer.

I watched two pit-sawyers at work like this in the Jaffna Peninsular of Ceylon, in about 1944. They were sawing the planks and timbers that were going into a sea-going brigantine being built nearby. She was a large ship and my imagination boggled when I considered the vast labour of having to rip down every timber and plank of her with what didn't look to me like a very high quality saw. The Bottom Sawyer, I noticed, was a very thin man, but – under his coating of sawdust – he seemed surprisingly cheerful! Perhaps some of us do not know how lucky we are.

The American colonists took with them from Europe the art of sawing timber with water-power. A water wheel would drive a simple crank which would cause a vertical saw blade to go up and down. The log would lay on a moveable trolley which would be pulled inexorably forward against the saw by a rope going over a pulley with a weight on the other end of it. It was easy to extend this by having several saw blades side by side and thus cut several planks or timbers out at once. This sawing must have been slow, but not so slow as the pit saw, and the device would need very little attention. The sawyer could let it get on with it and go away and do something else. It was safe, quiet, used no expensive fuel, and did not require much labour. Maybe sawmilling should have stayed right there.

—V—

CONSERVANCY
AND DEFORESTATION

THE VEXED question of whether to plant hard-woods or soft-woods is one that has exercised Mr Zetmayer for most of his working life.

Mr Zetmayer has recently retired from the post of Conservator of the South Wales forests of the Forestry Commission. He lives in a beautiful garden, on which he lavishes much attention, in a suburb of Cardiff. As Conservator he spent much of his time dealing with the politics of tree-planting.

The Conservator is responsible for all the government-owned forests in his area. He does not go into the forests with an axe or a planting spade but he sits in an office, tours around in a motor car, and attends meetings with all and sundry. He has to speak for the Conservancy's interests whenever these are involved.

Mr Zetmayer is very interested in the history of his profession. Where did the idea of Conservators come from?

"They came to Britain from the Indian Civil Service, but before that they came from France. I think the decree appointing *Monsieur le Conservateur* dates from 1798, and the first one was installed in 1801. As for India, it dates from when the German foresters went to India in the 1850s, and certainly by 1860 they were called Conservator. If you remember your Kipling you will recall that occasionally Mowglee meets a Forest Officer and they tend to be great men and they tend to be German. This of course interests me because my great grandfather came from Germany. He came from the Black Forest to Britain. The first Professor of Forestry in Britain, Professor Schlick at Oxford, was German by birth, German trained, and he served in India. He ended up with a knighthood.

"But my grandfather, who died in 1909, never had to change his nationality. He just moved to Britain in the course of business and he just stayed.

"My family was in the Black Forest and they owned a piece of forest in the mid-1800s that served an iron working and smelting business. It seems extraordinary for the very conservative small German states, but they were forestry pioneers. My grandfather left home to go to America via Italy, and I have a sporting gun which he was given in 1877 by the Grand Duke of Tuscany for his work in Italy with the Grand Duke's foresters and surveyors.

"The Germans were the great pioneers of forestry; but now they're looked upon as very conservative and traditional, and the French are much in the same mould. The more modern forestry movement is with the Swedes and the Danes. It was a German economist who first pointed out that the return on capital may be very small, and I know the economic theory is that if you are only getting two percent on your capital you should sell it off and invest in something more profitable. But of course what we have seen of inflation makes you think again! I have never really accepted the argument that Britain should have liquidated its forests several centuries ago. I know there are professors who agree with me that you should put them back, as it were, for once and for all through investment taxation, and *then* you should run them on a current profit-and-loss basis. I accept immediately that you should look at the interest implications when you decide courses of action. But I think the Treasury in Britain has come to accept the fact that the rate of return on forestry is low but *real*. The trouble is that no treasury or government really wants to back a business that takes fifty years before you get the full return."

This being so it is a miracle, perhaps, that any

forests survive in the British Isles. It is always more profitable to cut them down than to plant them.

"The old woods – the traditional woods in fact – lie on heavier soil which couldn't have been ploughed until the invention of the iron plough. By that time the landowners had found that they *liked* their woods. They liked the timber, they liked the sporting value – and they are really responsible for the traditional English landscape. I say English deliberately, because they particularly managed the land in a mixed way, for agriculture, for timber and for sport; they kept woods where perhaps even in their day it might have been more profitable to turn to agriculture.

"Wales and Scotland were different. The burning and clearances for sheep grazing destroyed the traditional woods. That they were once heavily wooded there is no doubt. This is well known from pollen analysis. You can show the time scale at which different trees arrived after the Ice Age, when probably tree cover in Britain was wiped out. First came birch and pine, and they were followed by other species, and then by oak. In the wetter periods willows and alders flourished more and in the drier periods there was pine. There are arguments still as to whether pine survived in southern Britain. The interesting thing is that even spruce was here before the Ice Age – it never got back before the Channel land bridge broke.

"I think forestry is an extraordinary activity. One of the Scottish professors said that it is unique among the activities of man, because the cycle of activities is not completed in the cycle of your life-time. Very few of the crops that I have seen planted

have been felled, and if they have it means that a mistake has been made. Around forty years is the shortest time – and I have been thirty-four years in the Commission. So if they have been felled at thirty-five it means something has gone wrong. I have been very lucky that while I have been in charge of things I have been able to cut timber that other people have planted and see it going to the sawmills. And I have seen the sawmill industry develop in Wales, along with other things. This has been one of the most exciting twenty years for seeing new industries.

"I think any forester must have the sense that he is planting for the next generation. It may sound a bit trite, but you are really doing something that, by and large, and with all the criticisms about how you do it, must be for the benefit of mankind.

Slowly, around the world, there is a growing awareness of the dangers of deforestation. The invention of the chainsaw has placed the power of felling the greatest of the forest giants in the hands of the feeblest and most stupid of men. You no longer have to be a Mr Penpraise or a Stan Ayres – men of might and sinew. Every country lad, if he can get one, gets a chainsaw now and our Sundays are raucous with the scream of these engines as they bring tree after tree crashing down. In the tropical jungles people who want to clear the forest don't bother to cut the trees down any more – they simply start great forest fires and burn them where they stand. Napalm bombing from the air is sometimes used by the huge ranching companies. I myself saw, in the jungle of eastern Sri Lanka, four tractors each as big as a house pulling a battleship's anchor chain through the jungle, cutting a swathe through the age-old trees a hundred yards wide as fast as a man could walk! This was for the cultivation of rice. The land they cleared is all abandoned now – eroded away. The jungle cannot return because there is no soil left. There are now no trees – no rice.

The Amazon jungles, after they have been burned, are sown with grass seed from the air. The thin laterite soil (all its goodness was burned with the trees) will support grass for ten or twelve years – enough to feed cattle for hamburgers and make a rich man richer. Then the soil goes too and leaves a desert.

The forests of Indonesia are being felled at a rapid rate by Japanese businessmen, to satisfy their country's apparently insatiable demand for chip-board. The same people have bought most of New Zealand's South Island rain forest to turn that into chip-board too, and the Japanese are buying up more and more of the Red Wood and Douglas forests of California. The Californian loggers win battle after battle with their government to be allowed to clear-fell yet more of their country's dwindling forests: forests which took thousands of years to develop and, once gone, will leave the soil beneath them to wash away too. In Africa, the goat – the desert-maker – destroys thousands of square miles of savanna forest every year with its teeth. So we should not quarrel with the British

Forestry Commission for covering some of our hillsides with conifers. As Mr Zetmayer pointed out, no other tree will grow there. Any tree is better than no tree.

But a few enlightened people throughout the world are trying to reverse the tide. Richard St Barbe Baker, with his Men of the Trees, has been the cause of millions of trees being planted. It's a drop in the ocean compared to the numbers that are being destroyed, but at least it is an attempt. My old friend Mr Mazibuko, in the Valley of a Thousand Hills in Zululand in Natal, is trying valiantly to get his fellow countrymen to plant trees on their devastated and eroded hillsides. He is having some success.* There are Friends of the Trees in the Himalayas who actually save the remains of the North Indian forests from being felled by passive resistance.

The men who have told us their stories in this book spent much of their lives cutting down trees, it is true; but what they were doing was perfectly respectable because they were farming the forests. The forests were not diminished by their activities. Listen to Mr Light again:

*If anybody wants to help him, a cheque to R.T. Mazibuko, PO Box 90, Plessislaer, Natal, South Africa, will buy a lot of trees.

"With hard wood – oak, and all that – you know it's a hundred years at least. I have planted a very good many! I can honestly say – and the wife will bear me out – that I have planted acres and acres of acorn, our own acorns off the Forestry Commission. But they have none at all now, and they have closed the nurseries down."

In England there are several organisations which are striving to save what is left of the world's forests. Herbert Giradet, who lives in the beautiful forest above Tintern because he loves forests, has been one of the principal founders of one of these.

"World Forest Action is a group that was started in 1979, because of the worsening situation in tropical forests – not just Brazil but in other South

American countries too. In Asia too the forests are under attack just as much as they are in South America. We are trying to arouse opinion among people in Europe in particular to the dangers of deforestation – and in particular when it is being perpetrated by Europeans and by European companies.

"It is certainly true that most of the beef produced on these short-term ranches in Brazil is being shipped to Europe, and in most cases it is being made into hamburgers. We have got to face up to the fact that we just can't afford to get rid of the immense treasure of tropical forests simply so that we can have more hamburgers to eat!

"It has been convincingly shown that more food can come out of these forests if they are alive and well than if they have been removed and replaced by ranches.

"World Forest Action has been trying to draw attention not only to the bitter facts of deforestation but also to the realistic alternatives. These alternatives can take many different forms. For instance we have taken up the campaign for Forest Farming, a method of farming where you use trees to produce annual crops. It can be done in tropical forest regions; it has been done and it has been shown to be successful. It is possible to harvest a vast range of proteins and carbohydrates, and all manner of fruit, either from the tropical forests themselves, or from plantations that have been established in tropical areas.

"This is what we might call a *permanent* form of agriculture, which is much more suited to tropical areas than the annual agriculture that we are used to in Europe. Here we have orchards of nuts and fruit, but the choice of fruit and nut trees over here is very limited: we only have ten or fifteen tree species which are suitable. In the tropics, on the other hand, the range is simply fantastic, and largely unexplored.

"We are trying to draw attention to the sheer scale of the destruction that is being wrought in the tropics – the most vulnerable region of the world today – and at the same time we are trying to point out alternatives to this destruction. Members of World Forest Action are working in re-afforestation in the Himalayas, in Peru and other places, and in Africa. We have tried to slow down if not halt this destruction.

"Forests are not just there for timber. Forests are there for a much greater variety of reasons, for example to ensure a continuation of the world's atmosphere. Trees breathe in carbon dioxide and breathe out oxygen, and if there are no forests then this process will be severely interrupted. The balance of the world's atmosphere is maintained by the forests and by the algae of the seas. Already there has been a dramatic increase of carbon dioxide in the atmosphere since the beginning of industrialisation. It has now been found that about half the increase has come from burning wood! A very considerable proportion of that comes from the burning of forests in the tropics.

"The second point is that where forests are removed one soon gets to the situation where droughts occur. In the Sahel region of Africa, for instance, there are very few trees left to hold the moisture, and as a result it has become increasingly difficult to graze cattle or carry on agriculture.

"The next very important point is the role of the forests in keeping the soil in place. This is particularly pronounced with mountain forests, and it has been found that the decimation of the forests of the Himalayas, both in India and Nepal and in all the Himalayan countries, is having serious effects on the agriculture downstream. The Himalayan forests, which used to act as a sponge during the periods of heavy rainfall and release the water slowly down-river, no longer fulfil that function. The water when it does fall gushes down-river and causes floods and landslides and is very detrimental to the plains of India. These are the ways in which forests are vitally and crucially important to mankind."

Herbert Giradet speaks for all of us who believe that life will be quite insupportable on this planet without the trees – spiritually insupportable as well as physically so.

"I have lived in or just on the edge of forests all my life. I am not a botanist or a forester, but when I see a wounded or a sick forest it makes my heart bleed. To see that great beauty and immense natural richness of forests disappear, on the scale at which it is happening, is terrible. The present rate of deforestation is quite unprecedented. Even if you look at the early stages of agriculture – in the Middle Ages, or even in Roman times – never have forests disappeared as fast as they are doing today. Realising these things I *must* involve myself!

"Once the soil goes, nature goes too. Ultimately we are going to be alone on this planet. Forests are the home of a vast number not only of plants but of other animals. Nowhere else will we find the variety of animals that there are in the forests. Even here, in the most uniform of forests, there is a tremendous variety of birds and so on. If you have ever heard the bird concert in the forest during early spring you realise this.

"The onslaught on the forests is probably worse than any other damage that is being done to nature in the world. Forests are so extraordinary defence-less. A tree cannot cry out. It will simply succumb to the chainsaw, and nowadays the technology of deforestation is absolutely devastating. They actually have machines that grab trees and pull them out by their roots, and there are other machines which just chew up the tree and make it into instant pulp. These are the sort of tools now commonly used. Nature and the forests are totally defenceless against this kind of thing.

"We should realise that the forests are the ultimate in God's creation. These are all the reasons why I feel I must be involved in these things, and in the struggle for the survival of the forests. It is not a struggle against something – it is a struggle for a new understanding about the relationships between man and nature. The forests are the greatest expression of nature's bounty."

What pleasure or glory could a man get from driving a machine that tears trees out by the roots, or that chews them up into pulp? What songs do such men sing?